T0378284

POVERTY
AND OUR FUTURE

GENE BROOKS

NEW YORK

Published in 2022 by The Rosen Publishing Group, Inc.
29 East 21st Street, New York, NY 10010

First Edition

Editor: Theresa Emminizer
Book Design: Michael Flynn

Photo Credits: Cover eric1513/iStock/Getty Images; (series background) jessicahyde/Shutterstock.com; p. 4 Igor Alecsander/Getty Images; p. 5 N. Pipat/Shutterstock.com; p. 7 Arnold Sachs/Archive Photos/Getty Images; p. 8 Pongkiat Rungrojkarnka/EyeEm/Getty Images; p. 9 Mario Tama/Getty Images; p. 10 ssguy/Shutterstock.com; p. 11 Anton_Ivanov/Shutterstock.com; p. 12 Snehal Jeevan Pailkar/Shutterstock.com; p. 13 Tony Karumba/AFP/Getty Images; p. 15 NurPhoto/Getty Images; p. 16 Dmytro Zinkevych/Shutterstock.com; p. 17 Mike Kemp/In Pictures/Getty Images; p. 19 Ali Yussef/AFP/Getty Images; p. 20 Reg Speller/Hulton Archive/Getty Images; p. 21 Fotosearch/Archive Photos/Getty Images; p. 23 Bennett Raglin/Getty Images; p. 24 Gideon Mendel/Corbis Historical/Getty Images; p. 25 Mark Sagliocco/Getty Images; p. 26 Pallava Bagla/Corbis Historical/Getty Images; p. 27 PETIT Phillippe/Paris Match Archive/Getty Images; p. 29 Kevin Hagen/Getty Images.

Library of Congress Cataloging-in-Publication Data

Names: Brooks, Gene, 1982- author.
Title: Poverty and our future / Gene Brooks.
Description: New York : PowerKids Press, [2022] | Series: Spotlight on
   global issues | Includes bibliographical references and index.
Identifiers: LCCN 2020011057 | ISBN 9781725324251 (paperback) | ISBN
   9781725324282 (library binding) | ISBN 9781725324268 (6 pack)
Subjects: LCSH: Poverty--Juvenile literature.
Classification: LCC HC79.P6 B676 2022 | DDC 362.5--dc23
LC record available at https://lccn.loc.gov/2020011057

Manufactured in the United States of America

CPSIA Compliance Information: Batch #CSPK22. For further information contact Rosen Publishing, New York, New York at 1-800-237-9932.

Find us on

CONTENTS

CHAPTER ONE

THE POVERTY PROBLEM

Would you be healthy if you didn't have enough food to eat? What if you got sick and you couldn't see a doctor? How good would your grades be in school if your home didn't have electricity? If you needed to work to help your family, could you even go to school? You might need to get a job, help your family farm, or search for clean water. These are daily problems for many people struggling with poverty, or the state of being poor.

About 8 percent of the world population lives below the international poverty line.

Many people in poverty must live on very little. Today, more than 600 million people live on less than $1.90 a day. This is known as the international poverty line. The United Nations (UN) has adopted a series of goals to help end extreme poverty by 2030.

CHAPTER TWO

A HISTORY OF POVERTY

For hundreds of years, most people believed that poverty was unavoidable. Some people said the poor deserved their situation. Some said people's life choices kept them poor. Some world leaders believed that poverty was necessary. They felt hunger could control people and keep them working.

Around the late 1700s, people began to realize that the way society was organized created poverty. They began to understand that many **institutions** help cause poverty. Working to end poverty became part of the goal of good governments.

In the 1960s, the poverty problem drew more attention in the United States. President Lyndon B. Johnson announced a war on poverty. Government policies addressed the troubles of poor families. This movement helped more people learn about worldwide poverty.

In 1964, President Lyndon B. Johnson signed a bill meant to reduce poverty in the United States.

CHAPTER THREE

TYPES OF POVERTY

Every country around the world has its own way of measuring poverty. The United States measures poverty by how much money people make. For example, Americans who earned less than $12,760 in 2020 were below the poverty line.

Some ways measure absolute poverty and relative poverty. According to the UN, absolute poverty is when people lack at least two of seven basic human needs. These needs include food, education, health care, and shelter. People also need clean water, **sanitation**, and the ability to get information.

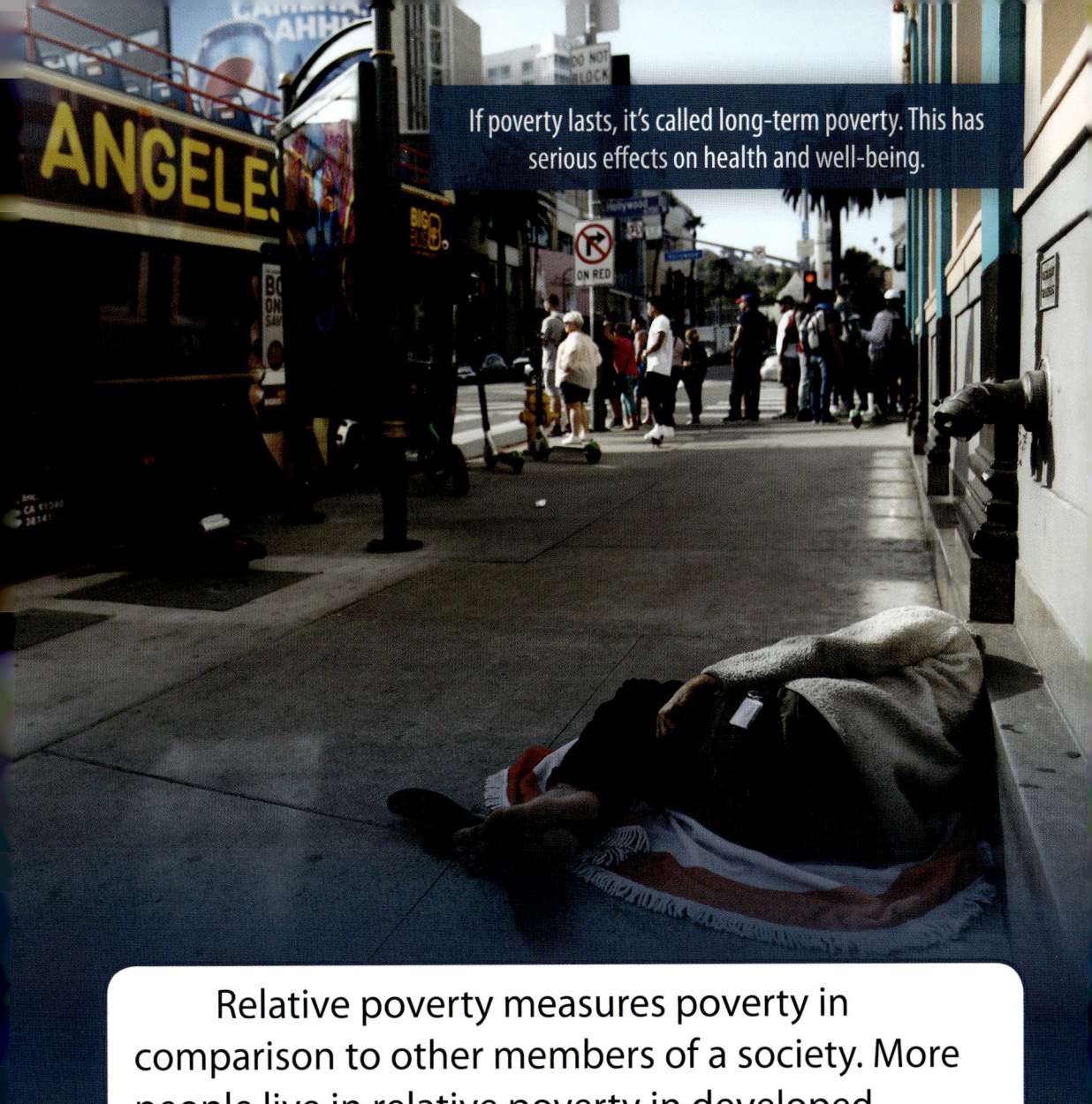

If poverty lasts, it's called long-term poverty. This has serious effects on health and well-being.

Relative poverty measures poverty in comparison to other members of a society. More people live in relative poverty in developed countries than live in absolute poverty. Many poor people in these countries have their basic needs met, but they have at least 50 percent less than others do.

CHAPTER FOUR

AROUND THE WORLD

Poverty is a problem around the world. Over the past 30 years, the center of extreme poverty has shifted from Asia to sub-Saharan Africa.

About 30 years ago, 1.9 billion people were living in extreme poverty. Over 1 billion of these people lived in India and China. However, economic growth and new social policies in these two countries mean that many people there are no longer living in extreme poverty.

Madagascar is a very poor country. More than 75 percent of the people there live in extreme poverty.

By 2018, extreme poverty had fallen to 650 million people. Many of these people lived in sub-Saharan Africa. In fact, more than half the people in that area lived in extreme poverty. The worst levels of poverty were in Nigeria and the Democratic Republic of Congo. If conditions don't improve, 500 million people around the world may still be living in extreme poverty by 2030.

CHAPTER FIVE

CAUSES OF POVERTY

All people need healthy food, clean water, health care, and a place to live. Those who don't have a way to get these basic **resources** can become poor. Sometimes this is because of **infrastructure** problems. Some areas may not have roads, bridges, or wells. All these things are meant to connect people with resources.

Natural disasters such as storms and floods can destroy much-needed resources. These events can affect people living in poverty more than other people and make poverty worse.

Activist Malala Yousafzai, center, works for the right to education, which can help people stay out of poverty.

Social and political differences can also create poverty. These things can prevent people from getting an education, and this lack can keep them from having an equal voice in their community or government.

Conflict or danger in an area can also help create poverty. Big conflicts such as war can destroy homes and infrastructure.

13

CHAPTER SIX

PEOPLE MOST AFFECTED

Poverty greatly affects children around the world. Children living in poverty are more likely to lack proper **nutrition** and become sick. In 2020, COVID-19 spread quickly all over the world. Not only did this increase the number of poor families, it took a heavy toll on poor children everywhere. Reports say the pandemic forced at least 150 million children into poverty.

Poverty affects women more often than men. Women earn an average of 24 percent less than men do. Women are also often more likely to do work that doesn't pay much, and they're often held responsible for unpaid work such as childcare and household duties.

People with disabilities are also more likely to be poor. They may have conditions that make them unable to work. Health-care costs can often lead to poverty.

More than 2 billion people lack clean drinking water in their homes. In some areas, girls and women often must spend their time searching for clean water.

CHAPTER SEVEN

SOLUTIONS FOR POVERTY

The UN has several goals to help people living in poverty by 2030. One goal is to get rid of extreme poverty. Another goal is to reduce the number of people living below national poverty levels by 50 percent. This includes improving social services that help people with hardships, providing equal access to resources and services.

Some antipoverty solutions hope to close the gap between what men and women earn.

Some antipoverty programs provide poor populations with help from outside their communities. A few of these projects include building wells and improving roads.

Other programs start among the community itself. They focus on what causes poverty and work to educate people. These efforts can lead to long-term improvements. Both kinds of programs can make a difference in solving worldwide poverty.

CHAPTER EIGHT

FIGHTING POVERTY

The fight against poverty also must include reducing inequality. In many countries, there are large gaps between social classes. These gaps include how much money people make and the opportunities available to them.

Inequality can lead to problems between groups. It often means that the poorest members of society can't reach their goals or become the best they can be. When everyone in a society can use similar resources and have similar opportunities, a nation can work better as a whole.

The World Bank is an organization that provides loans and grants to poorer nations around the world. It's meant to support the poorest members of society with government **reforms**. These reforms include providing young children with proper nutrition and providing everyone with health coverage and a good education. They also include improving roads and providing electricity.

If inequality is reduced, people will have a better chance to escape poverty.

19

Poor countries need the most help when working to reduce global inequality.

After World War II, the world's wealthier countries became more likely to offer help to developing countries. This became known as foreign aid. This aid helps countries that are struggling economically, sometimes during emergencies or natural disasters. Aid can help relationships between countries and protect human rights around the world.

In 1949, President Harry Truman announced a plan to help poor countries through foreign aid.

Foreign aid isn't always meant to change a nation's economy. Sometimes it's just meant to improve the conditions of the country's residents. It does this by focusing on services like health care or education. Some foreign aid solves short-term problems. This aid can still be very important and often life saving for people who need help quickly.

Most people living in extreme poverty don't have the resources to pay back large loans. In the 1970s, **economist** Muhammad Yunus made a plan to help solve this problem. Yunus and his bank began offering small loans called microloans. The loans were usually just a few hundred dollars or less. People could repay them in small amounts, often on a weekly schedule. This idea is called microfinancing.

Yunus created microloans to help poor people buy what they needed to start small businesses. Lenders hoped that these small businesses would bring people out of poverty. This doesn't always work. However, microfinancing is still an important tool for people today. People can use it to pay for emergency expenses and keep out of further poverty.

Muhammad Yunus's model of microfinancing began in Bangladesh. It's spread to many developing countries.

CHAPTER NINE

POVERTY AND CLIMATE CHANGE

Climate change has had negative, or bad, impacts around the world. It's had an especially rough impact on the poorest members of society. Climate change causes hotter global temperatures and rising sea levels. It also leads to worse storms and a drop in air and water quality.

Natural disasters push 26 million people into poverty every year. And by 2050, there may be 143 million people who have been forced to move because of climate change.

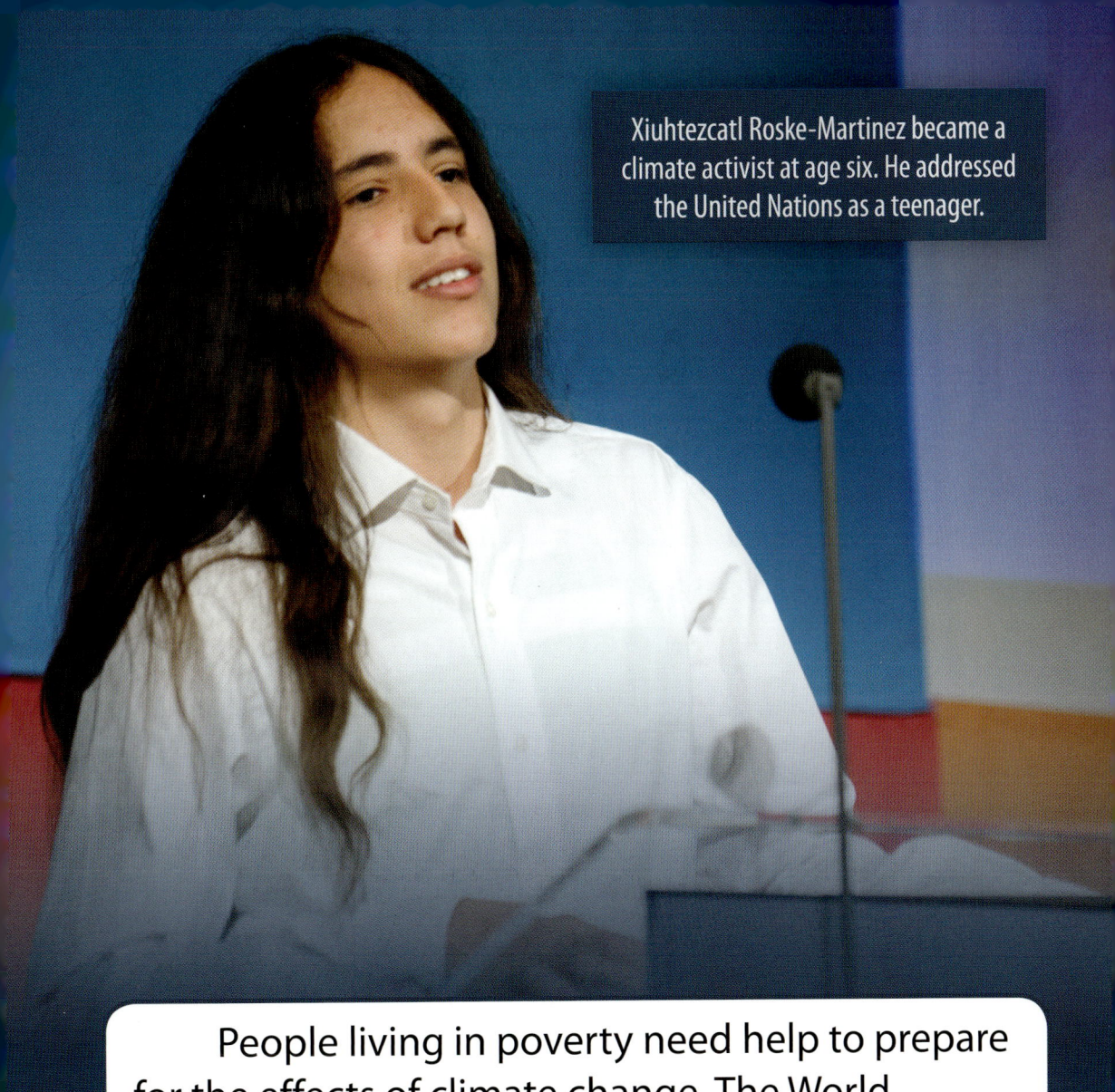

Xiuhtezcatl Roske-Martinez became a climate activist at age six. He addressed the United Nations as a teenager.

People living in poverty need help to prepare for the effects of climate change. The World Bank is helping those in poor communities build new homes and infrastructure that can stand up to natural disasters. In 2012, the World Bank helped the city of Beira, Mozambique, prepare for flooding with a new drainage system.

CHAPTER TEN

SOLUTIONS IN TECHNOLOGY

Technology can sometimes help reduce poverty. New developments may lead to energy sources that are better for the environment. Solar energy can provide power to poor people living in areas without other technology. Solar-powered stoves allow people to cook without wood fires, leading to better air quality. Solar water pumps can help provide clean drinking water. Solar-powered computers can help people get an education, which can be one of the best resources to help people out of poverty.

SOLAR WATER PUMP

A large solar power plant in Morocco may provide electricity to more than a million people.

Having a mobile connection can help people living in poverty stay connected with the rest of the world. Mobile phones can connect people to banking services and health care. They can receive emergency alerts and other important information.

CHAPTER ELEVEN

SOCIAL PROGRAMS AND POVERTY

Even people living in overall wealthy countries can experience poverty. A few years ago, Amika George of England learned that as many as one in 10 girls in her country didn't have the money to buy **menstrual** products. Many of these girls would have to skip school when they had their period. This is an example of how poverty can keep repeating. A lack of money keeps girls from buying period products, which also keeps them from going to work or school. These monthly breaks in work or education can push young women further into poverty.

To fix the problem of period poverty, George worked to make it easier for people to get menstrual products. At age 17, she started #FreePeriods. Her efforts grew into a large movement. Thousands of supporters donated money. In time, British lawmakers took notice of the #FreePeriods movement. In 2019, the government promised to make free menstrual products available in all high schools and colleges in England.

Amika George also tried to increase education about periods so people were more comfortable talking about them.

BILL & MELINDA
GATES foundation

GOALKEEP

—— Global Goals Awards 2C

CHAPTER TWELVE

HELPING SOLVE THE PROBLEM

The United Nations has declared that everyone has a basic human right to **dignity** and equality. People deserve life's basic necessities, including food, clothing, housing, medical care, and education. When people don't have these basic things, they're denied their human rights. This most often affects people living in extreme poverty.

Even you can help end poverty. You can help organizations that provide resources such as clothing and food for the poor. You can help out at homeless shelters or food banks. You can write letters to lawmakers asking them to help solve the poverty problem. You also can work to reduce climate change. Together, we can fight poverty at home and across the world.

GLOSSARY

activist (AK-tih-vist) Someone who acts strongly in support of or against an issue.

dignity (DIG-nuh-tee) The quality or state of being worthy of respect.

economist (ih-KAH-nuh-mist) Someone who studies economics, or the system or process by which goods and services are made, sold, and bought in an area.

infrastructure (IN-fruh-struhk-chuhr) The equipment and structures needed for a country, state, or region to function properly.

institution (ihn-stuh-TOO-shuhn) A custom, practice, or law that's accepted and used by many people.

menstrual (MEN-struh-uhl) Related to the periodic discharge of blood from females during menstruation.

nutrition (noo-TRIH-shuhn) The process of eating the right food to grow and be healthy.

reform (REE-form) A change to make something better.

resource (REE-sohrs) Something that can be used.

sanitation (sa-nuh-TAY-shuhn) The process of keeping places free from dirt and disease.

technology (tek-NAH-luh-jee) A method that uses science to solve problems and the tools used to solve those problems.

INDEX

PRIMARY SOURCE LIST

Page 7
President Lyndon B. Johnson holds up his "war on poverty" bill. Photograph. Arnold Sachs. August 20, 1964. Washington, D.C. Archive Photos via Getty Images.

Page 21
President Harry S. Truman sitting in White House library. Photograph. 1950. Washington, D.C. Archive Photos. Fotosearch via Getty Images.

Page 23
Muhammad Yunus. Photograph. Bennett Raglin. September 27, 2019. New York City. Getty Images Entertainment.

WEBSITES

Due to the changing nature of Internet links, PowerKids Press has developed an online list of websites related to the subject of this book. This site is updated regularly. Please use this link to access the list: www.powerkidslinks.com/SOOF/poverty